FADE
to
GRAY

FADE
to
GRAY

Anthony Black

To order additional copies of this book, contact:
Xlibris
1-888-795-4274
www.Xlibris.com
Orders@Xlibris.com
811737

CONTENTS

Foreword

In order to find ourselves on the other side of adversity and troubled times, we are forced – subconsciously, inadvertently – to narrow our minds and our vision. To focus only on the here and now, we are taught that in order to survive, we must set goals, keep a clear view of the minute things that will (we think) produce, in the end, a happy result. This is nonsense. Life is meant to be lived, without training wheels. Ride both the ups and the downs, they are both necessary to experience the totality of what life has to offer. We must know that we are never truly in control of our lives. There are too many unforeseen and uncontrollable variables, which produce inordinate amounts of anxiety and worry. Accept and embrace it. Life is best enjoyed with a yielding of control to whatever higher being you endorse.

We are but living embodiments of a ripple effect. We should content ourselves to cause a ripple, but not fret over the exact effects of said ripple. We incorrectly identify as the water, the shore, the animals, the plants, and even the sky. When in reality, we are but a leaf, destined to drop from a tree and land in a place that we have no more control over than how someone else lives their lives. No life in this world is more important than any other, there is no way to acquire any more value to your life, besides living as rightly as you possibly can.

This collection of poems and artwork was a means of relatively successful self-therapy throughout some of my darkest times. Each piece is an earnest attempt to quantify and articulate how difficult it has been to climb some of my life's tallest mountains, and learn to accept both the good and bad that have come with it. My hope is that some part of what this book offers, (and what it has already done for me) aids you in a fight that we **all in this world** share – depression.

Articulations of a man,
Sometimes swallowed by emotion
With a perfectly rational fear
Of being swallowed by the ocean

I breathe in deep,
And attempt to remember days past
Depression rooted Black
Unforgiven mistakes, I try to outlast

Now exhale slowly,
Own reflections in the mirror, either love it or hate it
There is no in between
Hold my emotions in check, to avoid being **naked**
A struggle, preferred unseen

Self Portrait

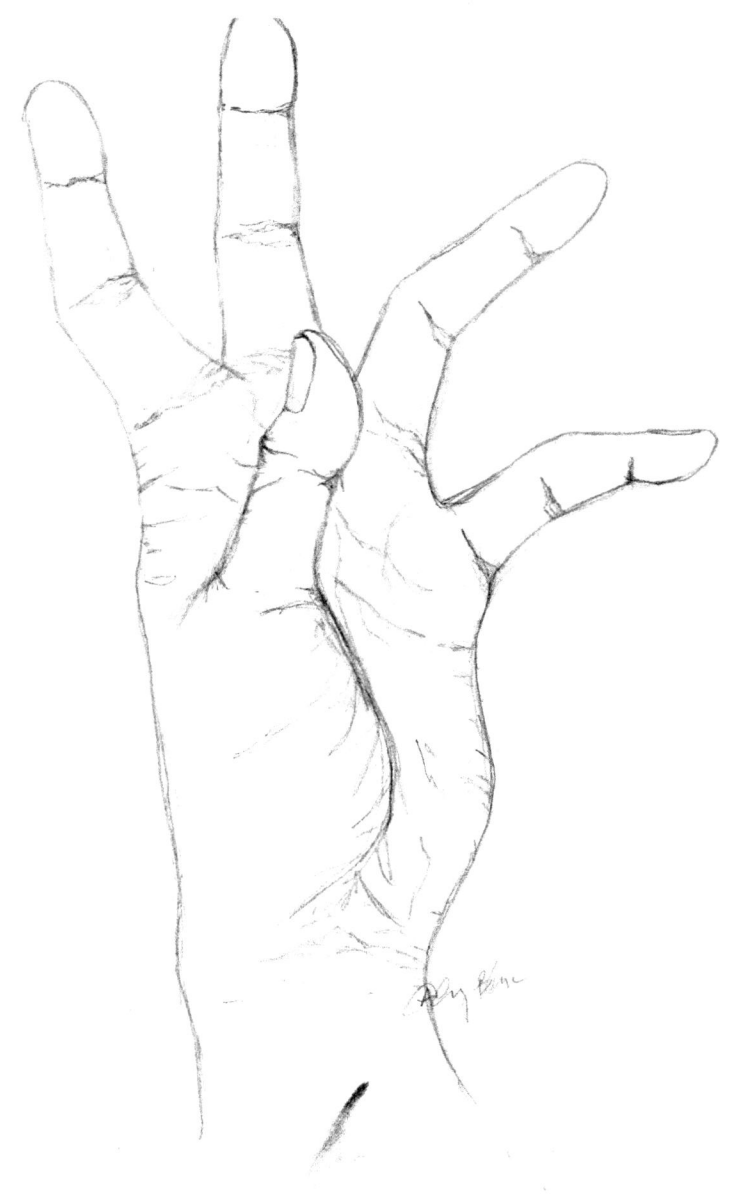

Something there
Just out of reach
Self-made barriers
Convinced I can't breach

My own motivations deceive
An inner manifest built in doubt
Limitations I alone weave

Claims of bystanding
As I shed control
Fear the sobering truth
Disguised as fire, I am charcoal

Blackened hands, assumed plight
A chosen perspective, focus on the black
Or, to create, and enkindle the light

Reaching

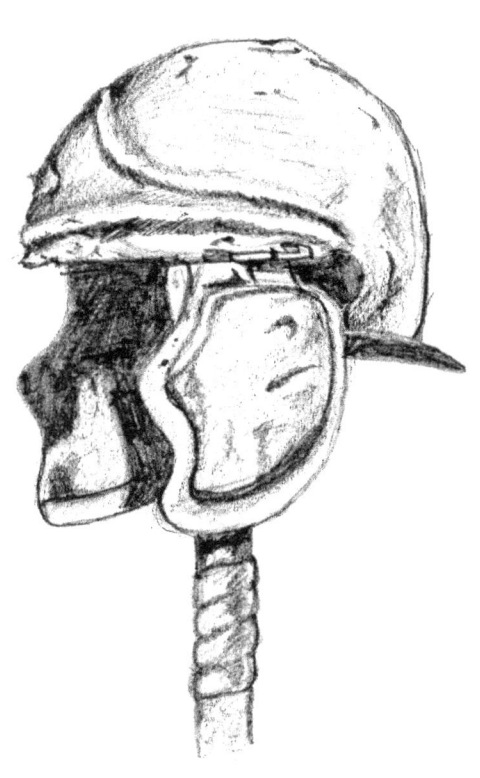

4

Hold on tight
Press it to your chest
Measure quickly
Refuse to invest

Obscure the view
Slant the conclusion
Here's another
Attempted intrusion

Calloused spirit
Broken down inside
Secrets withheld
Continue to hide

Guarded

Rebellious figments of my mind's creation
Routined pursuits ineffective of the situation
Isolation an enemy turned friend
Tunneled attempts to illuminate the end

A momentary reprieve
Silent darkness seeks to relieve

Convinced of the end, the world slows
A tense wait, as the pain quickly grows
Grounded, furniture a kindred spirit to **Everest**
A muted existence never so irreverent

Migraine

Poisoned pursuits to be well known
By people who don't know you
Discarded former selves left prone
By people desperate to be within view

A crater of missing purpose in life
Papered with ineffective bank notes
Which only serve to further our strife
Growing the emptiness until we're fully engrossed

Do your best to keep depression at bay
Only with our consciousness subdued
Lack of instant media creates dismay
Overloading information leaves us confused

Carefully constructed identity
Societal standards provides the mold
Unrecognized reflection, full of enmity
Unhappiness shines through, attempt to **remold**

Poisons

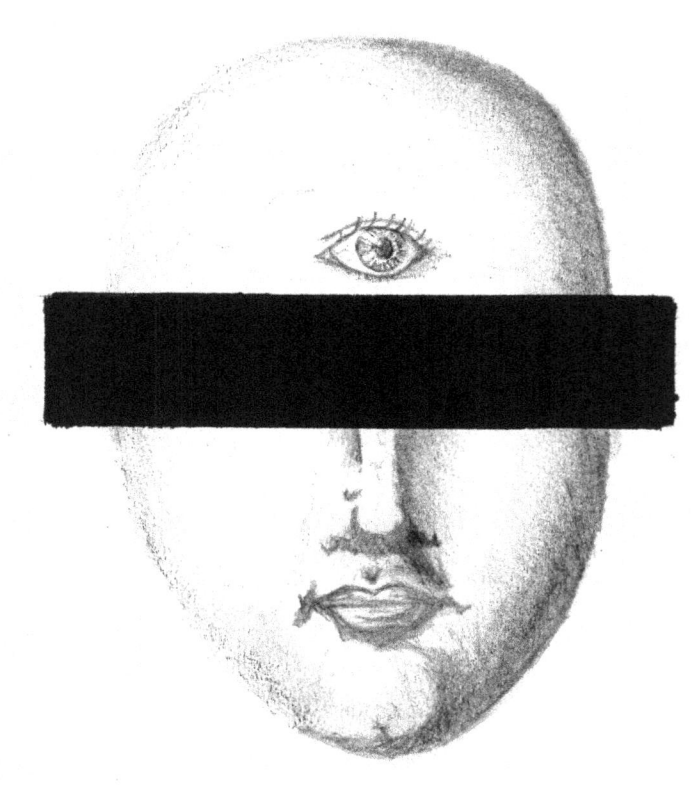

Assisted hallucinations dance in my peripherals
I sink in the couch with a focused dismissal
Silence exhausted, breathing turns abysmal
Lost in the tracks, followed trains run invisible

Sedated by the slow moving beats and tight-stringed vibrations
Senses and emotions coalesce in a dimly lit meditation
Purpose erased and redrawn with a heightened elevation
Future lives unchanged, dreams made with a medicated dedication

Empty plans and empty cans pile up in the corner
Return to Calvin Drive as an unrecognized foreigner
Desperate for escape, I stare down the corridor
Rising suns damage pride, any progress is **a forfeiture**

Faded

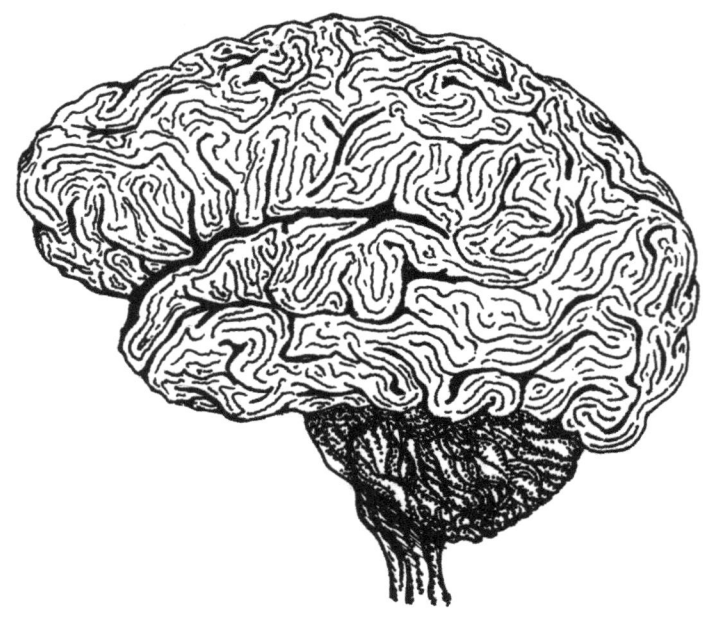

A willing prisoner to an expected system
Forsaken control, pretending wisdom
Routine is the master
And you, its deliberate victim

Change your face, fit the room
Contained self-interests, yet to bloom
The urge to please,
You recklessly consume

Routine

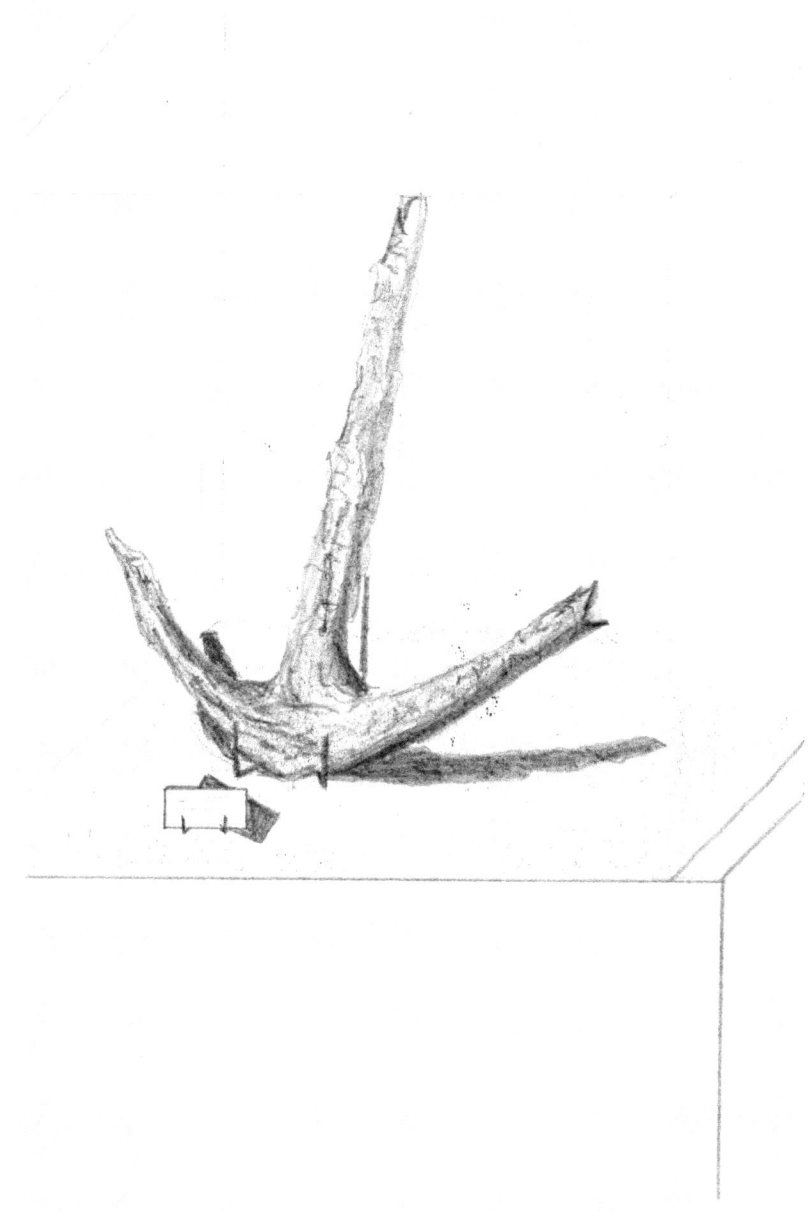

Anchored chains disguised as wealth
Coiled around your inviting spirit
Sedentary life numbing your mental health
Change portrays a monster, fear it

Dreams in your head are piped in reality
Dismissed by society, including you
Chasing is childish but desire causes duality
Feeling stuck shared by all but a few

Thoughts form, based on the collective
Interests suppressed in fear
Time wasted, introspection crosses **the directive**
Nature shaped in to a sorted career

Milestones

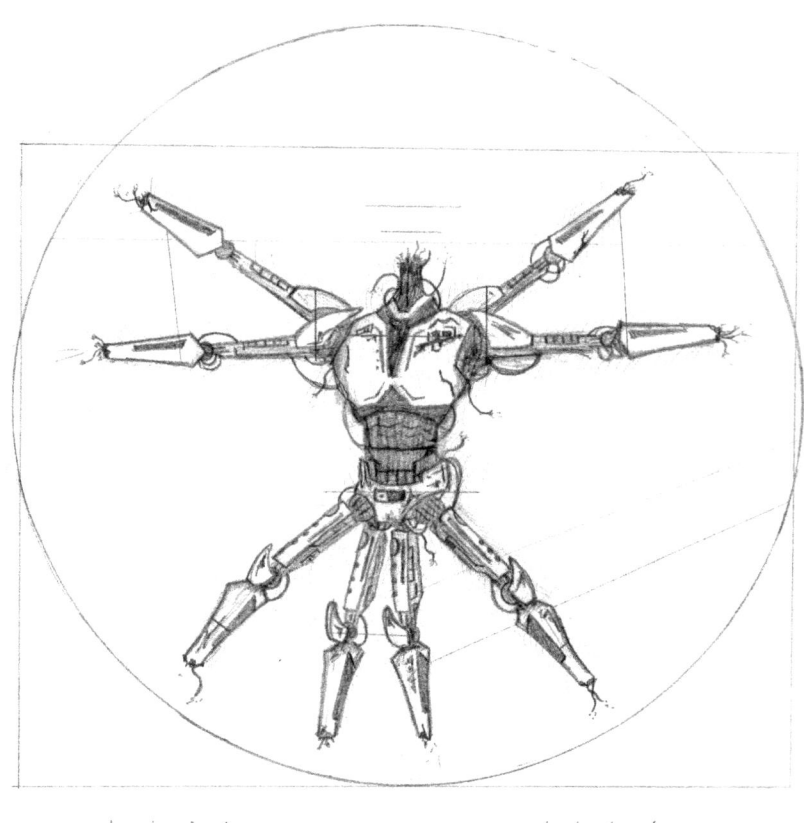

Heightened expectations
Without the ambition to achieve
Natural talents
Wither with the inclination to leave

Detached emotions
Built over a pride-less lifetime
Disappointed absence
Separate disappointment by a signed line

Inconsistent confidence
Masked over with zealous charm
A wild imagination
Encouraged to distract from internal **harm**

Self Portrait
(reprise)

Ever present, yet swallowed whole
Crowded around, within – alone

Methodically simple
An affectless ripple

Look up, ponder possibility
Now drop, drown in reality

Isolation

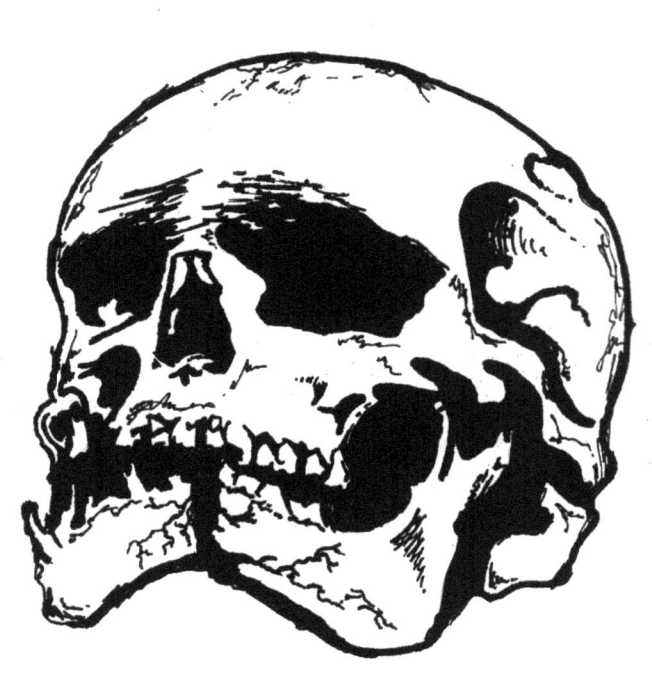

"I'm ready" forced through 3 am tears
Gone through the motions for 26 years

A smile and laugh dropped when doors close
No body left to find, an accident proposed

A world with me in it, is better without
I'll be forgotten quickly, I have no doubt

Just let me be in the wrong place at the wrong time
A distracted driver, a missed 'Wrong Way' sign

It'll be over in an instant, lacking in pain
A common event, no motive to **explain**

Twenty–Seven

One minute you were right
Beside me
Gone now and you left
My pride weak

This was a happy ending waiting to happen
Reality hit after you left me flattened
Is it something I said? Was it something I did?
Fake my own death
'Cause you left me on read

Lie on the ground and stare at the ceiling
Your silent response has left me reeling
My body melts in to the floor
Lack of movement, a carpet spore

Ghosted

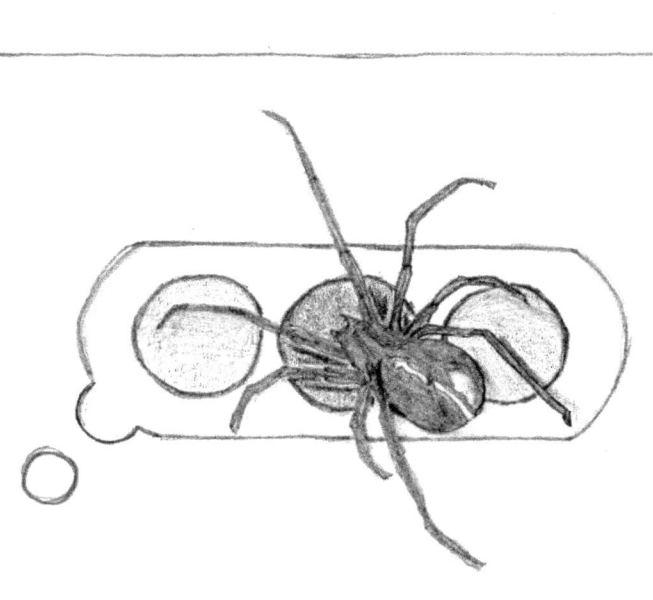

"**Hey** what's up?"

"Been a while since we chatted"

"Wanted to say hey"

"So that's why I added"

"You on Facebook so please"

"Just message me back"

Now stare at my phone

Until the screen turns black

Ghosted(pt.2)

Singular mountains, familiar tunnels
Clinging grip, unyielding struggle
Freeform chaos, relinquish control
Claiming freedom, creases unfold

Misguided importance, desperate ambition
Suppressed experience, favored repetition
Anxious openings, creating doubts
Forced company, avoided without

Tunneled escape, let it pass
Closed eyes, emotional impasse
Towered barriers, hidden behind
Faulted isolation, narrow mind

Tunnel Vision

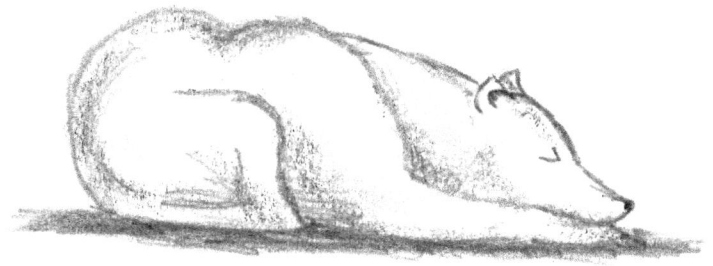

Squint your eyes and distort reality
Feign control and deny mortality
"This can't be real"
"This can't be happening"
The sun cannot conceal
The storm clouds are dampening

I cannot believe, I cannot accept
This gross indignation, I violently reject
Every ounce of me burns
With seething obsession
Remade memories return
In my mind, an infection

Reach out my hand,
Endlessly above
Purpose disguised,
Narrow-minded love
Offered exchange,
An attempted revision
She was beloved,
A laudable decision

The sun is now gone
The storm clouds persist
My willingness withdraw**n**
I no longer resist

Stages

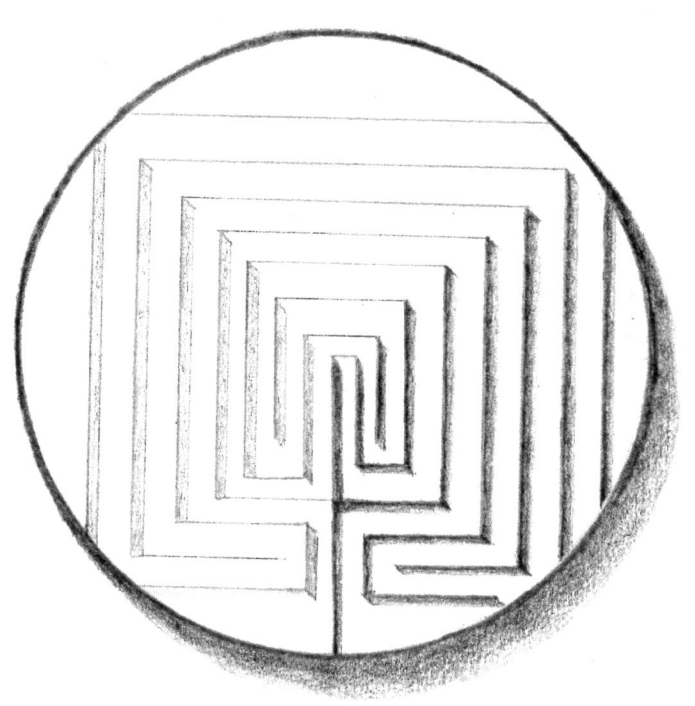

Walking through an empty field
Full of weeds
Picking at my insecurity
Until it bleeds

Stop and try to plant
Some confidence in the cracks of concrete
Frustrations shows
When it doesn't grow
Move on to something new **and repeat**

Impatient

In my mind, machinations of supposed perfection
I take ink to the outlines of my life
And attempt a permanent correction

Dismiss the positives of reality
To focus instead on the dramatic brutality
Pursue escape through created illusions
Given the choice of pills, take the blue ones

I choose to live in fabricated ignorance
Cling to the ghost of rose-tinted memories
Close in the borders, live a life of **immanence**

Perfection

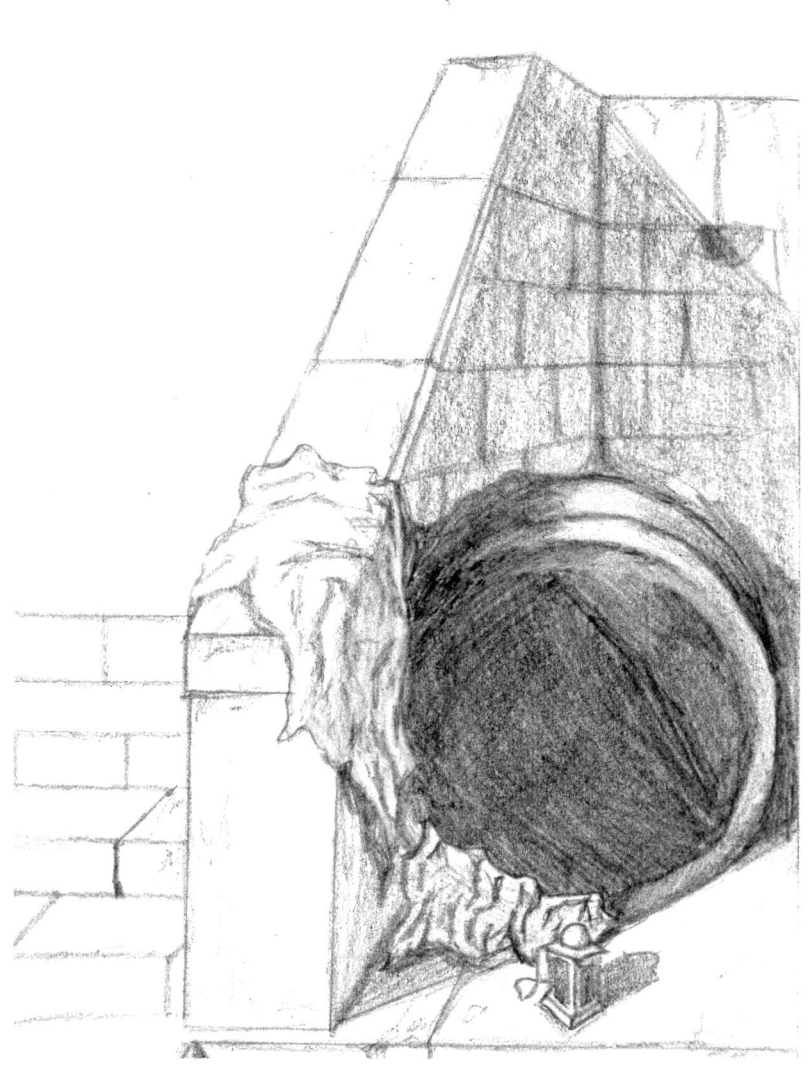

A falsely confident ambling
Upon
A fence that is straddling
On one side sits
The existential terror of night
Tense filled anticipation
Of a sudden drop in flight

I dip my toe
Fighting internally
To resign in to
The void eternally

The thought of you drags me back
Unrelenting to the blackness
You are a hint of sane
Within an engulfing madness

Atop the fence I return
To wade between
The devouring sadness
And the slightly less obscene

With you by my side
My near perfect compliment
I begin to slowly lose
The 'falsely' from my confident

A Thin Line

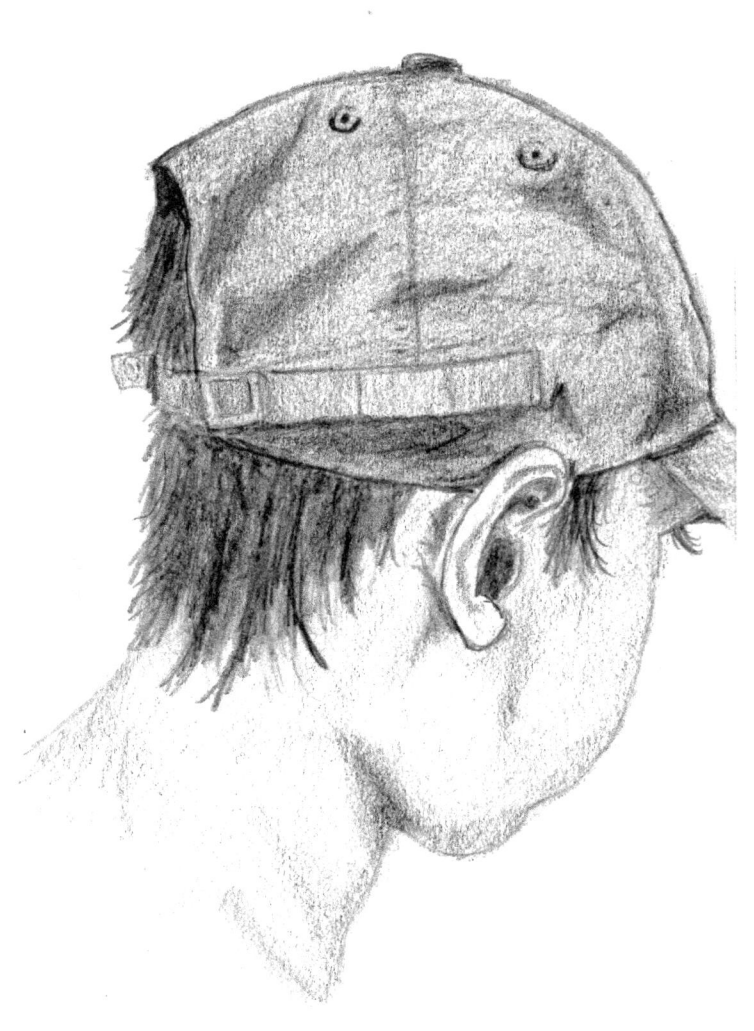

Twisted and contorted in unique ways, but broken down we're all just DNA
We all just go through the motions of a life put in front of us without being engaged

Illusions of power fueled by the number of zeros in our bank account
Fame is celebrated as the peak of human existence, as followers of celebrities we are devout

An air of eminence increases its potency as you watch the number of followers grow
Superficial wealth and material goods attempt to fill emotional cracks like a round peg in a square hole

No human being is above or below any other and is only granted that feeling of entitlement when they are able collectively fool the masses into believing that they are better.

We are all just slightly obscure realizations of the same **concept.**

DNA

What is the sun to an ant?
What is a flower to a tree?
What is the moon to the sand?
What is a road to a leaf?

What is your life to another?
Who is your harshest critic?
Who does your depression smother?
Who defines all your limits?

Who does a comparison benefit?
Build yourself, and after all you've **done,**
Who will disassemble it?

Comparisons

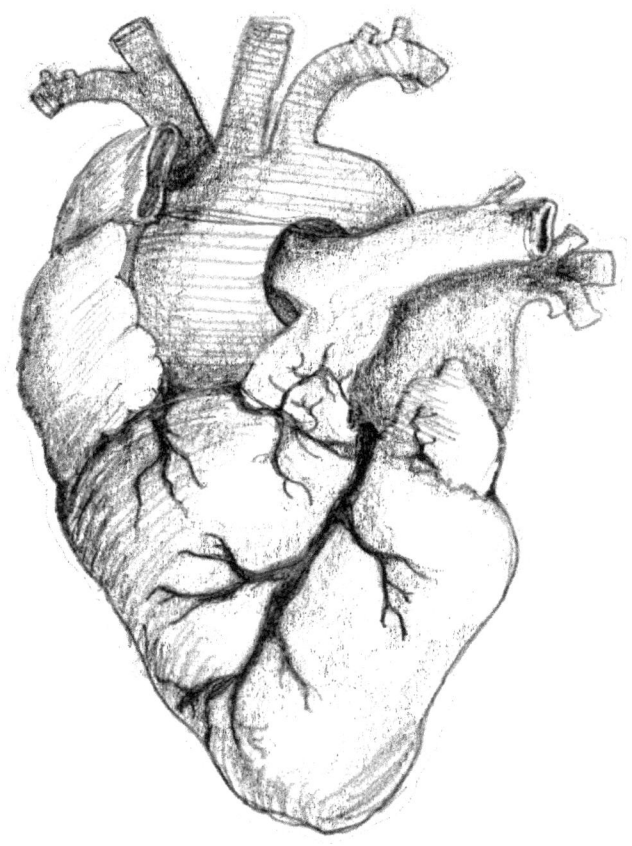

Meander down the path of least resistance
Shrug aside any feelings of persistence
Master in the art of deflection
Residence on the back burner
To prevent the crushing weight of rejection

Inner focus left in the past
Revisit and watch suppressed pain rehash
Compulsively obsessed with opinions
Insignificant particulars
Drag the mind away from decisions

Untitled

She is chapstick on a dry lip
And coming home after a long trip
Stray into the void and she brings me back
She is the answer to everything I lack

She is individual among the generic masses
Standing out further and further as time passes
She is an unlikely result of a likely source
Her smile renews life in this walking corpse

The world is a tempest and she is my shelter
Favored as I'll ever be when I have held her
I am a labyrinth and she is my solution
She is clarity in a world of confusion

She Is

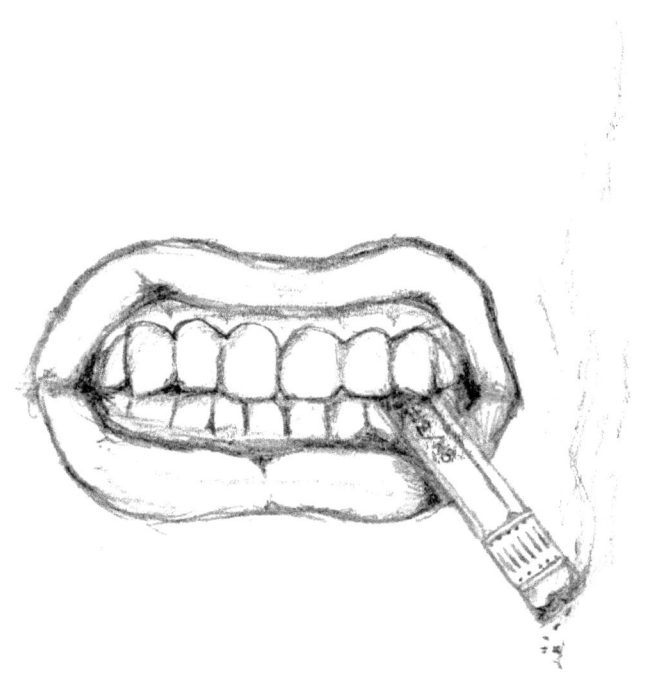

Affirmations, whispered under-breath keep me conscious
Stare in the mirror until I convince myself it's Adonis
Flaws abundant as I contend with my own objections
Mental warfare on home soil, battle to change perceptions

Rehearsed confidence hides a villain that preys on me alone
Untended garden in my mind with weeds overgrown
Hands on either side, pulling myself up again and again
Pray above for strength to fight, lose it when I say 'amen'

Your best ally is the one who stares back at you from across
The mirror reveals the conductor of your thoughts
Twisted and worn, attempting to convince you of **a false view**
So shout those affirmations back if you have to

Self–Love

We are but leaves on a freshly green tree
We look down on our lives and weep
Rewards of other trees we'd reap
A promise of fulfillment others refuse to keep

I am one of many, given every tool to thrive
Instead I merely survive
I see the sun, and refuse to face it
I feel the wind, but refuse to embrace it

A careless, wishful leap we take
To the cold ground, our lives we forsake
A changed perspective for which we've yearned
A brown, decayed existence is all we've **earned**

Perspective

Afterword

When writing each of these poems, I drew from very specific situations and personal relationships in my life and how they affected me. While reading them, I hope you can relate them to your own life in a way that is unique and specific to you. If you ever wish to share your story, I implore you to express yourself in whatever way gives you the most amount of peace, as this book has done for me. And if you would like to hear more of what each piece means and the inspirations behind each drawing and poem, I welcome any questions you may have to the email listed below, and will respond as timely as my current mental state **will allow.**

anthony.e.black52@gmail.com

Lightning Source UK Ltd.
Milton Keynes UK
UKHW010706240520
363742UK00004B/124/J